Living Responsibly in an Age of Excuses

Whatever Happened to Moral Responsibility?

by
Anthony M. Coniaris

LIGHT & LIFE PUBLISHING
MINNEAPOLIS, MINNESOTA

Light and Life Publishing Company
P.O. Box 26421
Minneapolis, MN 55426-0421

Copyright © 1999
Light & Life Publishing Company
Library of Congress Card No. 98-75813

All rights reserved. No part of this book may be reproduced, stored in a retrieval system, or transmitted in any form or by any means, electronic, mechanical, photocopying, recording, or otherwise without the written permission of Light and Life Publishing Company.

ISBN 1-880971-43-7

Preface

Living Responsibly in an Age of Excuses is based on Psalm 51. It is for this reason that we begin this book with the words of Psalm 51. Almost every worship service of the Orthodox Church includes this great psalm which is one of the finest expressions of repentance and confession ever written.

Table of Contents

Who Me?	Page 1
How It All Started	Page 1
Not So Admirable Pattern for Human Behavior	Page 3
What Would Have Happened If . . .?	Page 5
His Anger Was Within Him	Page 5
Victimology	Page 6
Lessons From a Cartoon	Page 7
The Cold Air	Page 8
The Winning Jockey	Page 9
The Blame Game	Page 11
"The Fire Made Me Do It"	Page 12
Condoning Criminal Conduct	Page 13
"Mob Violence Made Me Do It"	Page 14
The "Spanish" Disease	Page 15
No Fault Insurance	Page 16
Passing the Buck	Page 17
Scapegoating	Page 17
"It's the Teacher's Fault"	Page 19
The Blame Game Again	Page 20
Jesus Came to Stop the Blame Game	Page 20
The Twinkie Defense	Page 22
Your Genes Are to Blame	Page 23
"My Parents Made Me Do It"	Page 25
"My Environment Made Me Do It"	Page 28
"Poverty Made Me Do It"	Page 29
"I'm Not Responsible Because I'm Sick"	Page 32

"I'm Compulsive, Addicted!"	Page 34
Smoking - An Addiction?	Page 35
"It's My Bad Luck!"	Page 37
"God Made Me This Way!"	Page 38
"The Devil Made Me Do It"	Page 39
"Hitler Made Me Do It"	Page 42
Why We Do It!	Page 43
Stealing the Sermon	Page 44
"I am Eichmann!"	Page 46
"I'm Only Human!"	Page 48
I Am Responsible	Page 50
Our Inability to Accept Responsibility	Page 50
We Make Choices For Which We Are Responsible	Page 52
Man: A Self-Excusing Animal	Page 53
A Statue of Responsibility	Page 55
Choices Are Important	Page 56
Blame Yourself	Page 57
The Lighter Burden	Page 59
Pride Edits Truth	Page 60
When Two People Have a Quarrel	Page 61
"Father, I Have Sinned."	Page 62
David's Greatness: His Confession	Page 64
Where Does the Buck Stop Ultimately?	Page 65
Admit It!	Page 67
Coming Face-to-Face with God	Page 68
From the Canon of St. Andrew of Crete	Page 69
He Stole Heaven	Page 70
When Is Man a Failure?	Page 71
Prayer	Page 73

Psalm 51

- Have mercy on me, O God, according to thy steadfast love according to thy abundant mercy blot out my transgressions.
- Wash me thoroughly from my iniquity, and cleanse me from my sin!
- For I know my transgressions, and my sin is ever before me.
- Against thee, thee only have I sinned, and done that which is evil in thy sight,
- so thou art justified in thy sentence and blameless in thy judgment.
- Behold, I was brought forth in iniquity, and in sin did my mother conceive me.
- Behold, thou desirest truth in the inward being; therefore teach me wisdom in my secret heart.
- Purge me with hyssop, and I shall be clean;
- wash me, and I shall be whiter than snow.
- Fill me with joy and gladness; let the bones which thou hast broken rejoice.
- Hide thy face from my sins, and blot out all my iniquities.
- Create in me a clean heart, O God, and put a new and right spirit within me.
- Cast me not away from thy presence, and take not thy holy Spirit from me.
- Restore unto me the joy of thy salvation, and uphold me with a willing spirit.
- Then I will teach transgressors thy ways,
- and sinners will return to thee.
- Deliver me from bloodguiltiness, O God,
- thou God of my salvation,
- and my tongue will sing aloud of thy deliverance.
- O Lord, open thou my lips, and my mouth shall show forth thy praise.
- For thou hast no delight in sacrifice; were I to give a burnt offering, thou wouldst not be pleased.
- The sacrifice acceptable to God is a broken spirit;
- a broken and contrite heart, O God, thou wilt not despise.
- Do good to Zion in thy good pleasure; rebuild the walls of Jerusalem,
- then wilt thou delight in right sacrifices, in burnt offerings and whole burnt offerings;
- then bulls will be offered on thy altar.

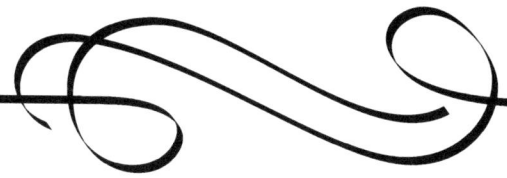

Who Me?
〜

- A person walked into a psychiatrist's office one day with his head wrapped in strips of bacon and an egg on top of the bacon.

- He sat down and said to the psychiatrist,

- "I'm here to talk to you about my friend. He has a problem."

- How easy it is to see other peoples' sins, not our own.

- When the teacher asked Johnny one day to name two pronouns, he replied with the following two pronouns: "Who, me?"

- These two pronouns, "Who, me?" have always served as a ready and easy denial not only of reality but also of responsibility.

- Contrast this attitude with that of David in Psalm 51:

- *For I know my transgressions and my sin is ever before me.*

How It All Started
〜

- Our modern world is very fond of passing the buck, of evading responsibility.

- It all began long ago, way back in the Garden of Eden.

- When Adam was asked by God why he sinned, he said to the Lord,
- "The woman, whom Thou gavest to be with me, she gave me fruit of the tree, and I ate."
- "It was on account of the woman you gave me!" said Adam.
- He blamed not himself but two other people: his wife and God!
- Then, when the Lord said to Eve,
- "What is this that you have done?"
- She replied, "The serpent beguiled me, and I ate."
- It was all the fault of the serpent.
- Husbands and wives have been blaming each other ever since: "It's not my fault; it's yours..."
- It is interesting that the consequences of the Fall of Adam and Eve were:
    1. Shame and embarrassment.
    2. They hid from God.
    3. Their relationship with God was broken.
    4. They blamed each other. The man blamed the woman. The woman blamed the serpent and the serpent didn't have a leg to stand on!
- This was certainly not the attitude of David who blamed no one but himself:
- *For I know my transgressions and my sin is ever before me.*

NOT SO ADMIRABLE PATTERN FOR HUMAN BEHAVIOR

- It certainly seems that Adam and Eve set the pattern for human behavior, and the pattern has not changed much since their day.

- We get ourselves into fixes of one sort or another and then we look around for someone or something to blame for our troubles.

- Of course, we're careful to take all the credit for our virtues and achievements;

- It's only for our sins and faults that we look for someone to blame.

- We hold ourselves responsible for our virtues.

- The only thing we are not responsible for is our failures and mistakes.

- When things go wrong we offer modern versions of Adam's complaint.

- The husband says, "The woman Thou gavest me, she is driving me to distraction."

- The wife says, "The husband Thou gavest me, he's driving me out of my mind."

- The harried mother says, "The children Thou gavest me are ungrateful. They're making me miserable."

- The incompetent workman explains his failure by saying, "The foreman has it in for me."

- The lazy student says he "flunked" because, "My Math teacher didn't like me."

- Another person blames his unhappiness on the fact that "My mother never really loved me."

- And on it goes endlessly.

- We look for scapegoats and we ride them for all they are worth.

- We blame our ancestors.

- We blame our biological and emotional make-up.

- We blame the changing times.

- We blame our circumstances.

- It is so much easier to fix blame than to fix problems.

- We even use—or rather misuse—psychology to convince ourselves that sin is no longer sin, it's a sickness for which we are not responsible.

- We blame everybody but ourselves.

- We forget that when we point the finger at someone else, one finger is pointing to the other person, but three fingers are pointing right back at us.

- A professional investigator of airline accidents said that the biggest obstacle to discovering the cause of an airplane crash is a surviving pilot who is always rationalizing and offering excuses.

WHAT WOULD HAVE HAPPENED IF . . .?

- What would have happened if Adam and Eve had repented?
- St. Symeon the New Theologian says,
- "Had they repented, they would not have been expelled.
- They would not have been condemned.
- They would not have been sentenced to return to the earth from which they had been taken."
- Instead, God said to them, "Dust you are and to dust you shall return."

HIS ANGER WAS WITHIN HIM

- The Desert Fathers tell the story about the monk who decided that he was making no spiritual progress in the monastery.
- He told the other monks that they were holding him back, constantly doing things that made him angry, which, of course, interfered with his prayer.
- But when the monk had left and was settling in a cave of his own, looking forward to perfect peace,
- he became frustrated over some trifle and threw a water jug against a wall, breaking it in pieces.

- Realizing that his anger was within him, and that it would be with him wherever he went, he returned to the monastery, apologized, and was taken back.

- *For I know my transgressions and my sin is ever before me.*

VICTIMOLOGY

- John Leo wrote,

- "We are deep into the era of the abuse excuse.

- The doctrine of victimology—claiming victim status, meaning you are not responsible for your actions—is beginning to warp our legal system . . .

- Juries have traditionally been very tough on excuses.

- Now the trial revolves around excuses.

- Traditionally, defense lawyers tried to create doubts.

- Now they just place the actual victim on trial,

- as they did in the Menendez trial."

- The same happened in the O.J. Simpson trial as well.

- Alan Dershowitz, one of O. J. Simpson's attorneys, said about the trial, "Now you're going to see the defense brutally attacking these victims. By the end of this trial, nobody's going to have a kind thing to say about the two dead people."

- In other words, they had it coming.

Lessons From A Cartoon

- Let me share with you a "Calvin and Hobbes" strip by cartoonist Bill Watterson.

- In the first frame, while trudging through the snow, Calvin declares to Hobbes, "Nothing I do is my fault."

- In frame two, the little boy stops to explain, "My family is dysfunctional and my parents won't empower me! Consequently, I'm not self-actualized."

- Frame three depicts Calvin in a pious pose as he continues his explanation, "My behavior is addictive, functioning as a diseased process of toxic codependency! I need holistic healing and wellness before I'll accept any responsibility for my actions!"

- The final frame has Calvin stomping off triumphantly as he declares, "I love the culture of victimhood."

- To which Hobbes replies, "One of us needs to stick his head in a bucket of ice water."

- We need more than a bucket of ice water.

- We need to confess as David did,

- *For I know my transgressions and my sin is ever before me.*

THE COLD AIR

- One person said about cold weather:

- "Last year the temperature got down to 45 degrees below zero and the wind blew at 35mph.

- That gave us a wind chill temperature of 108 below zero.

- Brrr. That's cold!

- The TV weatherman said that we had low temperatures because cold air was coming down from Alaska.

- When I heard that, I thought to myself,

- 'Strange. Whenever something bad happens, we blame someone else.'

- I'll show you what I mean.

- When I lived in the United States, the weatherman said the cold air came from Canada.

- I live in Canada now and the weatherman says the cold air comes from Alaska.

- When I lived in Alaska, they said the cold air came from Siberia.

- It always seemed to come from somewhere else."

- What lesson do we get from this but that

- the bad things we blame on others.

- The good things we have no trouble taking credit for.

- David could have blamed his sin on his prosecutor, the prophet Nathan (2 Sam. 12:1-23).

- But when Nathan said to David, "You are the man,"

- David said in Psalm 51,

- *Against Thee, Thee only have I sinned, and done that which is evil in Thy sight.*

- It was when David accepted responsibility for his sins and repented that he experienced the joy of salvation.

THE WINNING JOCKEY

- The "winningest" jockey in the history of horse racing was paralyzed in a tragic accident when he drove his car off an embankment.

- Today he's a quadriplegic confined to a wheelchair.

- And who's to blame?

- Well, this man and his lawyers filed a flurry of lawsuits.

- They sued the hospital where he was taken.

- They sued the doctors.

- The sued the highway commission for not installing guardrails.

- Their list of whom to sue even included the company that built the vehicle he was driving.

- Everybody's to blame except the man himself.

- Apparently the fact that he was legally drunk at the time of the accident had nothing to do with it.

- That's an extreme case of the victim mentality.

- Another example:

- A person was fired for being consistently late for work, despite repeated warnings.

- He sued his employer, claiming that he suffered from an ailment called, "chronic lateness."

- He claimed further that under the 1973 Rehabilitation Act he deserved to be reinstated to his job.

- He won.

- In another case, an inebriated person jumped in front of a subway train.

- He sued on the grounds that the engineer should have stopped sooner.

- The result?

- He wound up with a $600,000 judgment.

The Blame Game

- People love to play the blame game, blaming everyone but themselves.

- "Road rage" has now been classified as a sickness.

- This means you are not responsible for it.

- If you caught AIDS through drug needles or promiscuous sex, blame society for not doing enough in the fight against AIDS.

- If you committed a crime that landed you in prison, blame the people around you for getting you in trouble.

- If you've got a drinking problem, blame it on your nagging wife and on too much pressure at work.

- And if all else fails, blame God.

- Some people never go to church or pray, but when things go wrong and they need someone to blame, God suddenly comes to mind.

- Tornadoes and earthquakes are called "acts of God."

- How often is a beautiful sunrise called an "act of God?"

- There are prison inmates and drug addicts and women with unwanted pregnancies who find their situation very difficult and who then proceed to ask how God could let such things happen to them.

- In the victim mentality, God has no right to judge you for your sin, but you have every right to judge God for not making life pleasant for you in spite of your sin.

- Contrast this with David who blamed no one but himself:

  - *For I know my transgressions and my sin is ever before me.*

"THE FIRE MADE ME DO IT"

- We read in *Ex. 32:24:*

- "So they gave it [the gold] to me: then I cast it into the fire and there came out this calf."

- In the story from which these words are taken we see Moses go up into the mountain to hold communion with God.

- While he is gone the Israelites begin to murmur and complain.

- They want other gods of their own.

- Aaron, the brother of Moses, is their priest.

- He yields to the people, and when they bring him their golden earrings he makes out of them a golden calf for the people to worship.

- When Moses comes down from the mountain he finds the people deep in their idolatry.

- Moses is indignant. He destroys the idol.

- Aaron is frightened at what he has done.

- Like all timid men, he trembles before the storm which he has raised.

- And so he tries to persuade Moses, and perhaps in some degree even to persuade himself, that it is not he who has done this.

- He lays the blame upon the furnace.

- "All I did was throw the earrings into the fire and out came the golden calf."

- Contrast Aaron's behavior with David, who when confronted with Nathan's "You are the man," confessed, and took full responsibility for his sin.

- *For I know my transgressions and my sin is ever before me.*

CONDONING CRIMINAL CONDUCT

- Supreme Court Justice Clarence Thomas wrote:

- "An effective criminal justice system—one that holds people accountable for harmful conduct—simply cannot be sustained under conditions where there are boundless *excuses* for violent behavior and *no* moral authority for the state to punish.

- If people know that they are not going to be held accountable because of a myriad of excuses, how will our society be able to influence behavior and provide incentives to follow the law?

- A society that does not hold someone accountable for harmful behavior can be viewed as condoning—or even worse, endorsing—such conduct."

"Mob Violence Made Me Do It"

- A large part of the problem is that criminals today no longer face the sure punishment they once did.

- A few years ago a violent criminal was awarded $4.3 million in New York.

- Why?

- He had mugged and almost killed a 72-year-old man, then fled the scene.

- A police officer shot the criminal in the back;

- the courts deemed that wrong and awarded—rather rewarded the criminal with 4.3 million dollars.

- Public reaction? Virtual silence.

- Other court cases have proved similarly disheartening.

- During the Los Angeles riots, Damian Williams and Henry Watson were filmed pulling an innocent driver out of a truck,

- crushing his skull with a brick and doing a victory dance over his fallen body.

- Their lawyers then built a successful legal defense on the proposition that people cannot be held accountable for getting caught up in mob violence.

- When the trial was over and these men were found not guilty on most counts,
- the sound heard throughout the land was relief instead of outrage.
- Who me? No! No! I just got caught up in mob violence! Mob violence made me do it.
- Whatever became of moral responsibility?

THE "SPANISH" DISEASE

- A certain Dr. Roback made a collection of international insults.
- He discovered that by the French, syphilis was termed "the Spanish disease,"
- by the Spanish, "the Italian disease,"
- by the Italians, "the French disease,"
- each nation placing the blame on another nation.
- Whatever happened to moral responsibility, the kind David expressed when he said,
- *Against Thee, Thee only have I sinned, and done that which is evil in Thy sight.*

No Fault Insurance

- Some years ago a new concept was introduced into the insurance business.

- It was called "no-fault" insurance.

- The idea was that if something happened, nobody would be held accountable.

- That way property damage could be settled without going through the difficulty of determining who was at fault in causing the accident.

- From no-fault insurance we went to no-fault divorce.

- And no-fault has now become part of our culture.

- Retired General Colin Powell said,

- "We live in an age that is sick with what someone called *victimism*.

- Everyone is a victim.

- No one accepts responsibility for one's behavior.

- 'It's not my fault,' is the overriding excuse."

- If David had said, "It's not my fault" there would have been no forgiveness. Instead, he accepted responsibility for himself and said,

- *Against Thee, Thee only have I sinned, and done that which is evil in Thy sight.*

- Then it was that God restored to him "the joy of salvation."

Passing the Buck

- An easy way of not facing up to faults has always been the art of scapegoating, putting the blame on others, passing the buck.

- Will Rogers once named the three ages of America as:

- the passing of the Indian,

- the passing of the buffalo, and

- the passing of the buck.

- Passing the buck has become almost a worldwide pastime.

- It takes a very strong man, and also a very perceptive one, to have a sign on his desk as Harry Truman did, saying,

- "The buck stops here."

- *For I know my transgressions and my sin is ever before me.*

Scapegoating

- "Scapegoating," literally, "putting all the blame on a goat" comes from Leviticus 16:20-22:

And when the priest has made an end of atoning for the holy place and the tent of meeting and the altar, he shall present the live goat, and confess over him all the iniquities of the people of Israel, and all their transgressions, all their sins; and he shall put them upon the head of the goat, and send him away into the wilderness by the hand of a man who is in readiness. The goat shall bear all their iniquities upon him to a solitary land; and he shall let the goat go into the wilderness.

- Who is the real scapegoat?

- Jesus, of course! He became a scapegoat for you and me.

- He assumed my sins and yours.

- He forgives me when I repent.

- And if He forgives me, then I can forgive myself.

- I can relax and not go around blaming others, justifying myself, alibiing, and being defensive.

- I am at peace with God and with myself.

- If we are going to scapegoat, let's do it right.

- Take it to Jesus.

- He gave us a sacrament for it called Confession.

- "If we confess our sins, God is faithful and just and will forgive our sins and cleanse us from all unrighteousness," wrote the Apostle John.

"It's The Teacher's Fault"

- Have you ever overheard students discussing the results of their exams?

- One says, "I got an *A*";

- the other sulks, "He gave me an *F*."

- Human nature?

- Yes!

- We tend to blame others for our failures, "He gave me an F," and ourselves for our successes,

- "I got an *A*."

- Who me? No! It's the teacher's fault. She didn't like me. She gave me an F.

- The fact is that a person is never a failure *until* he blames someone else.

- Then he's a real failure with no chance for improvement.

- To be a real person is to be responsible, to accept responsibility for one's actions.

- *Against Thee, Thee only have I sinned, and done that which is evil in Thy sight.*

- *Whoever sees his sin is greater than he who resurrects the dead,* said St. Isaac.

- Such a person does resurrect the dead — the "dead" person being himself.

THE BLAME GAME AGAIN

- Although the Blame Game is a popular game, it is a highly injurious one.

- Here's why:

- Blaming others never heals—it always hurts.

- Blaming others never makes people whole in their relationships—it only breaks relationships.

- Blaming others never unites—it only divides.

- Blaming others never builds—it only tears apart.

- Blaming others never solves a problem—it only compounds the problem.

JESUS CAME TO STOP THE BLAME GAME

- Jesus came to stop the Blame Game.

- In response to his disciples who wanted to know who was to blame, who was at fault, Jesus said,

- "Why do you see the speck that is in your brother's eye?

- Or how can you say to your brother, 'Let me take the speck out of your eye,' when there is a log (a 2x4) in your own eye?

- You hypocrite, first take the log (the 2x4) out of your own eye, then you will see clearly to take the speck out of your brother's eye" *(Matt. 7:3-5).*

- "If you think your brother has a splinter in his eye, you're not seeing properly," said Jesus.

- "You're the one who has a serious eye ailment because you've got a log in your eye!

- You're the one who is blind!

- You've got the problem!

- You need to focus your attention on yourself, not on your brother," Jesus was saying.

- Abba Anthony said to Abba Poemen,

- "This is man's chief work: always to blame himself for his sins in God's sight."

- Abba Poemen said,

- "When asked what he is doing in his cell, the monk can briefly reply, 'I am weeping for my sins,'

- for the monk must always have *penthos* (sorrow) in his heart."

- Sorrow for one's own sins.

- There is no end to the Blame Game, until, like David, we confess,

- *Against Thee, Thee only have I sinned and done that which is evil in Thy sight.*

- *For I know my transgressions and my sin is ever before me.*

THE TWINKIE DEFENSE

- Have you heard of the "Twinkie Defense?"

- Dan White, the disgruntled city employee who shot the mayor and city supervisor of San Francisco, raised what became known as the "Twinkie Defense."

- He committed the murders, he said, because he was temporarily insane from a junk-food sugar high.

- And then there was the case of a doctor arrested just outside of Washington, D.C.

- A state trooper stopped the physician after watching her car weaving across the road's center line.

- The officer and his partner noted alcohol on her breath, and when they tried to take her in for testing, she kicked one of the troopers in the groin.

- Later, at the county jail, she drop-kicked the breath analyzer across the room.

- But in court the judge ruled her not guilty.

- Her successful defense?

- She was suffering from premenstrual syndrome!

- If we are victims of PMS or crack or sexual addiction or racism or whatever, then something or somebody else is always to blame.

- Americans have the highest per capita representation of lawyers in the world and spend $117 billion a year on insurance to protect against litigation.

- Who me? No! It was Twinkie or PMS! They made me do it!

- Whatever happened to moral responsibility?

YOUR GENES ARE TO BLAME

- The cover of *Time* Magazine (Aug. 1994) had this caption:

- "Infidelity: It May Be in Our Genes."

- We've heard it many times:

- "My genes made me do it."

- Perhaps there is also a rape gene and a murder gene.

- Someone said,

- "Heredity is a splendid phenomenon that relieves us of responsibility for our shortcomings."

- One person who is doing research on the ethical implications of genes wrote:

- "The molecular biologists and other genetic researchers with whom I work overwhelmingly agree that, regardless of what the genes do, we as individuals are still responsible for what we do.

- Genes are not dictators.

- We are not puppets, not mere servants, not ants carrying out genetic mandates.

- Environmental factors and individual experience play an important role in gene expression."

- And, most importantly, so does the human will.

- We are not determined or controlled genetically, but we do inherit a genetic predisposition which can be resisted by God's grace.

- Our whole nature, including the genetic part, has been damaged by sin, making us susceptible to many passions.

- But this act is no excuse for sin since we still have room for moral choices.

- We have all been dealt a different genetic hand in life, but we are each responsible for how we play that hand.

- Who we are as a person is more than merely our genetic and environmental influence.

- So, we cannot excuse ourselves by saying, "Sorry, my genes made me do it."

- We should not grant genes more power than they deserve.

- Violence is not in my genes.

- It is in my free will.

- This is what makes violent behavior a sin.

- If violence is a sin—the result of a wrong moral choice—then what a wonderful freedom we have.

- If we have sinned, we are free to repent and by God's grace, we can be set free.

- Tertullian's words speak powerfully to us about our genes and passions:

   We read that "the flesh is weak," and we thereby soothe our consciences at times. Yet, we also read that "the spirit is strong" (Matt. 26:41). For both expressions occur in the same sentence. Flesh is an earthly material. Spirit is a heavenly one. Why then are we so prone to make excuses for ourselves? Why do we offer our weak part as our defense? Should we not rather look at our strong part? Why shouldn't it be the earthly that yields to the heavenly? Since the spirit is stronger than the flesh, being of a nobler origin, it is our own fault if we follow the weaker of the two.

"My Parents Made Me Do It!"

- Another excuse is:

- "My parents are to blame!

- If you only knew the kind of family I was raised in, you would understand why I break my commitments and think of no one but myself."

- You've heard it and you keep hearing it again and again:

- "My father never cared about me.

- That's why I am what I am."

- "My mother made all kinds of mistakes in bringing me up.
- It's her fault."
- "My parents did not love me.
- That's why I turned to crime."
- It's always been a fad:
- Letting Mom and/or Dad have it.
- And, as someone said,
- "A society full of victims is a bunch of people who have a free pass not to take responsibility for their actions."
- The Menendez case, for example, is only one of many recent trials in which high-powered attorneys used "victimology," in this case, blaming the parents, to manipulate the juries.
- Let me share with you this humorous poem by Anna Russell:

    I went to my psychiatrist
    to be psychoanalyzed,
    To find out why I killed the cat
    and blackened my wife's eyes.
    He put me on a downy couch
    To see what he could find,
    And this is what he dredged up
    From my subconscious mind:

    When I was one, my mommy hid
    My dolly in the trunk,

*And so it follows naturally,
That I am always drunk.*

*When I was two, I saw my father
Kiss the maid one day,
And that is why I suffer now—
kleptomania.*

*When I was three, I suffered from
Ambivalence toward my brothers,
So it follows naturally,
I poisoned all my lovers.*

*I'm so glad that I have learned
The lesson it has taught,
That everything I do that's wrong
Is someone else's fault!*

- Gilbert Chesterton graciously absolved his parents of all responsibility for his behavior when he wrote in his autobiography:

  I regret that I have no gloomy and savage father to offer to the public gaze as the true cause of all my tragic heritage; no pale-faced and partially poisoned mother whose suicidal instincts have cursed me with the temptations of the artistic temperament ... and that I cannot do my duty as a true modern, by cursing everybody who made me whatever I am. I am not clear about what that is; but I am pretty sure that most of it is my own fault.

- As in all of his writing, Chesterton adhered to his belief that each individual is responsible for his or her own decisions as well as their consequences.

- Who me?

- Of course not! It was my dad, my mom. They had it in for me.

- Whatever happened to moral responsibility?

"My Environment Made Me Do It!"

- B.F. Skinner, a leading exponent of the idea that man is not free to make moral choices, in his book *Beyond Freedom and Dignity* sets forth his argument for concluding that the sole determinant of human behavior is environment.

- According to him, a human being does not "act upon the world," but "the world acts upon him" and determines his every decision.

- The choice, he says, is made for us, and we are powerless to act contrary to the way we've been pre-programmed.

- According to this view, the criminal is not responsible when he breaks the law—it's the fault of his background and society.

- Skinner concludes that the only way to improve our world is to change the conditions into which people are born and live.

- We would like to ask Professor Skinner just one question:

- How come Adam and Eve who lived in the Garden of Eden—the most perfect environment that ever existed—how come that perfect environment did not prevent them from sinning?

- And how about the person who said,

- "I was born in the slums but the slums were not born in me"?

- Created in the image of God, man has the free will and the grace of God to rise above any and all kinds of environments.

- It's not so much society but human nature that needs to change.

- Once human nature is changed by God's grace, then it will create a better society and environment.

"Poverty Made Me Do It!"

- In the 1950's a psychologist, Stanton Samenow, and a psychiatrist, Samuel Yochelson, sharing the conventional wisdom that crime is caused by environment, set out to prove their point.

- They began a 17-year study involving thousands of hours of clinical testing of 250 inmates in the District of Columbia.

- To their astonishment, they discovered that the cause of crime could not be traced to environment, poverty, or oppression as they believed.

- Instead, they discovered that crime is the result of individuals making, as they put it, wrong moral choices.

- In their 1977 work *The Criminal Personality*, they concluded that the answer to crime is a "conversion of the wrong-doer to a more responsible lifestyle."

- In 1987, Harvard professors James Q. Wilson and Richard J. Herrnstein came to similar conclusions in their book *Crime and Human Nature*.

- They determined that the cause of crime is lack of proper moral training among young people, particularly during the morally formative years, of ages one to six.

- In other words, the crime problem boils down to concepts foreign to our understanding today.

- The root of our crime problem is the loss of individual morality and the resulting erosion of our character as a people.

- George Bernard Shaw said,

- "People are always blaming their circumstances for what they are.

- I don't believe in circumstances.

- The people who get on in this world are the people who get up and look for the circumstances they want, and, if they can't find them, make them."

- When President Lyndon Johnson declared war on poverty, the message went out that the poor were unable to extricate themselves from their plight.

- In a landmark speech at Howard University in 1965, he told black students that they were the victims of society's oppression and racism and that their government would rescue them.

- LBJ, his compatriots in Congress, and the socially conscious elite who championed the war on poverty were well intentioned.

- They really believed that institutional programs could solve poverty.

- They really believed that the poor were victims.

- Unfortunately, they were also very convincing.

- Up until then the work ethic had been strong among the inner-city minorities.

- Now all that changed.

- *If my condition is not my doing*, the minorities now reasoned, *then why work to try to get out of it?*

- And if society is at fault, then why not steal from society?

- Why not let society support me?

- After all, I'm a victim of society!

- As long as people think this way, they will never get up and make something of themselves.

- David's conversion began when he accepted responsibility for himself and said,

- *I know my transgressions and my sin is ever before me. Against Thee, Thee only have I sinned.*

"I'M NOT RESPONSIBLE BECAUSE I'M SICK!"

- Others use the excuse, "I'm not responsible because I'm sick."

- One psychologist wrote about blaming sickness for your condition:

    Are you sick? If not, then something is wrong with you. You are sicker than you think. In fact, you are sick, sick, sick. Everyone is sick. So is everything. People are sick, dogs are sick, movies are sick, books are sick, towns are sick, governments are sick, the whole world is sick.

    We sympathize with the sick. We tolerate their symptoms. We give them tender, loving care. We want them to get well. But I am sick of everything and everybody being sick! sick! sick!

    Today everything and everybody is sick simply because everything and everybody falls short of being perfect. Every impropriety, every breach of decorum, every incident of unseeming conduct is a symptom of sickness... The disobedient, ill-mannered, rebellious child is a sick child...He must not be scolded for being sick...nor punished for having symptoms. He doesn't need discipline. He needs tender, loving care because he is sick, sick, sick.

    Juvenile delinquency is a sickness, and vandalism is its cardinal symptom. It is important that the delinquent not be held responsible for what he does, lest he develop a guilt complex. Feeling guilty is a worse sickness than delinquency, and no one wants the delinquent to be any worse than he is.

Criminals are sick. It is barbaric to incarcerate them in penal institutions. They belong in hospitals where they can be served by pretty nurses, entertained by doting volunteers, and absolved of all wrong by the magic of a psychiatric diagnosis.

Alcoholism is a sickness, and the alcoholic is a sick man. Alcohol makes him sick. It isn't what he does to alcohol, it's what alcohol does to him. Don't blame the drunk. Blame the drink.

Furthermore, since the diagnosis absolves him of all responsibility for himself, he makes no effort to improve himself. He is content to remain sick sick, sick.

I am sick of this kind of sickness. I am sick of its symptoms. I am sick of misbehavior being reinforced under the guise of therapy. I am sick of the whole mess. I am sick of sick, sick, sick.

- Dr. William Kilpatrick, noted psychologist and professor, wrote,

  There is ample evidence that the phenomenon Christians call "slavery to sin" does, in fact, exist. You may, as is the modern habit, call it what you like, but there are reasons not to remove the label. The words sin, repentance, and forgiveness all imply freedom and responsibility. When you take away those labels, you very often take away freedom and responsibility as well. Now this is what has happened by and large. We have taken the phenomenon of slavery to sin and renamed it "sickness."*

- Whatever became of moral responsibility?

---

* *Psychological Seduction: The Failure of Modern Psychology.* William K. Kilpatrick, T. Nelson Publishers, Nashville 1983. p.82.

- How much we need to imitate David's repentance and confession:

- *I know my transgressions and my sin is ever before me. Against Thee, Thee only have I sinned and done that which is evil in Thy sight (Psalm 51).*

- *He who sees his sin is greater than he who resurrects the dead,* said St. Isaac.

"I'm Compulsive, Addicted!"

- A court found that an FBI agent who embezzled $2000.00 and lost it in an afternoon of casino gambling was not a criminal.

- He was rather "a victim of Compulsive Gambling Syndrome" and was reinstated on the job.

- There are those who say that they can't help it because they are compulsive.

- People blame many sins on their compulsions.

- There is only one thing wrong with this argument:

- every action performed under compulsion always points back to the moment when I sold myself to that compulsion;

- the moment when, acting as a free person, I walked up to it, offered it my hand, sold myself to it, and enslaved myself to it.

- The other excuse, besides compulsion, is that, "I can't help it. I'm addicted."

- When baseball star Wade Boggs was caught in adulterous affairs several years ago, he explained that he was just a victim of sexual addiction.

- Similarly, Pete Rose claimed that he was addicted to gambling.

- Former mayor of Washington, D.C., Marion Barry used the same defense, but with a new twist.

- When he was filmed by the FBI with his hand in the cocaine jar, he claimed he was the victim of a racist plot.

- Militant gay activists suffering from AIDS rarely acknowledge that their disease might be a consequence of their own behavior.

- Instead, they angrily blame the government for not finding a cure.

- Whatever happened to moral responsibility?

SMOKING - AN ADDICTION?

- Almost 30 percent of U.S. adults are smokers.

- Most are said to be addicted, a term that suggests they have lost control and cannot help themselves.

- Yet we know that most of the 40 million ex-smokers in the United States today quit without official treatment.

- They decided to quit—and did so.

- I'm not suggesting we shouldn't try to help people quit their self-destructive habits.

- But the first step toward a cure is to remind them that they have the power to help themselves.

- The greatest power on earth is the power of the human will aided by God's grace.

- We will continue to lose the war on drugs as long as we view addiction as only a medical problem.

- It is basically a moral problem.

- People choose to become addicts.

- They can also choose by God's grace to overcome their addiction.

- Malcolm X once said,

- "If you get knocked down to the ground by someone else, that's not your fault.

- But if days and weeks pass, and you're still lying there, that is your fault."

- Who me? No! It's my compulsion, my addiction!

- It was not a compulsion or addiction for David. It was a sin for which he assumed full responsibility.

- *Against Thee, Thee only have I sinned and done that which is evil in Thy sight.*

"It's My Bad Luck!"

- Many times we blame our failures on bad luck.

- "Just my luck!" said a woman who had three unhappy marriages.

- "I'm so unlucky in love," she said.

- Yet each time she picked a man with an alcohol problem.

- Luck is largely the result of taking appropriate action.

- When we're passive, when we don't take sufficient charge of our affairs, we're victims of all sorts of bad luck.

- As one woman said, "I have noticed that the harder I work, the luckier I seem to be."

- There is a Greek proverb that says that we create our own luck—good and bad.

- Once you recognize your own role in creating less-than-perfect situations, you are able to make changes.

- That's when things get better.

- Where fate, destiny and luck are concerned, all of us have been given certain resources, abilities—and disabilities.

- What you do with what you've got helps determine your luck.

- "The fault," as the Shakespearean quotation goes, "is not in our stars, but in ourselves."

- The more we act to change our luck, the more we take charge, the "luckier" we become!

"GOD MADE ME THIS WAY!"

- Another excuse often used to pass the buck is the following:

- "God made me this way."

- I can hear God thundering from heaven:

- "Did I make you to be a thief, an adulterer, an addict, a libertine, or did I create you to be my son or daughter, created in my own image and likeness, with the gifts of free will and grace so that you may choose Me and find life?"

- Someone said so well,

- "We blame God for the harvest when we do the sowing."

- How often do we hear excuses such as:

- "If God had been doing a better job—if God had given me better people to work with—I'd have done better.

- God shouldn't have put me in that situation.

- After all, God knows I don't do well with those kind of people.

- After all, I'm only human."

- Or we hear people blaming God in ways like this:

- "God, You are the real problem!

- You could have prevented me from getting into this mess."

- Or maybe our thinking takes this turn:

- "I prayed about what I did, and if it was wrong, surely the Lord could have kept me from doing it."

- I've even heard people shrug their shoulders and say,

- "I didn't choose to be born!"

- St. James writes,

- "Let no one say when he is tempted, 'I am tempted by God'; for God cannot be tempted with evil, and He Himself tempts no one; but each person is tempted when he is lured and enticed by his own desire" (James 1:13-14).

- Who me?

- Of course not! Don't you know that God made me this way?

- Whatever became of moral responsibility?

"THE DEVIL MADE ME DO IT!"

- Another excuse is, if God didn't make me do it,

- "The devil made me do it."

- This is exactly what Eve said when she pointed to the serpent:

- "The serpent deceived me" (Gen. 3:13).

- St. John Chrysostom jumps in here and says,

- "She (Eve) did not say, 'The serpent *forced* me and I ate.'

- Instead what?

- The serpent *deceived* me.'

- In other words,

- She had the choice of being deceived and not being deceived."

- And so it is: we always have a choice.

- The devil can never force us.

- All he can do is provide the temptation, not the sin.

- We sin when we yield to Satan.

- Sin is our response to Satan's suggestion.

- Never can he force or make us do anything against our will.

- Following is a humorous story about "the-devil-made-me-do-it":

- A woman went on a shopping spree and came home with a beautiful but expensive dress!

- Cautiously, she showed the lavish purchase to her husband.

- But when he heard the price, he threw up his hands in horror and asked,

- "How could you do it!?"

- "The devil made me do it," she answered.

- "But," her husband continued, "why didn't you do as it tells you in the Bible and say, "Get thee behind me, Satan?"

- "I did," she coyly replied, "and I heard him say to me,

- "It looks beautiful, dear, even from behind."

- The buck stops right where you are, said the apostle James.

- "A person is tempted when he is drawn away and trapped by his own evil desires.

- Then his evil desire conceives and gives birth to sin;

- and sin, when it is full-grown, gives birth to death" (James 1:13-15).

- Mark the Hermit put it this way:

- "Neither is it Satan, nor is it the sin of Adam, but we ourselves who are to blame."

- And until we acknowledge our responsibility that the fault is not in the devil or God or in our compulsions or in our addictions,

- but in us, there will be no repentance, no healing, no forgiveness, no salvation.

- Repentance is, above all, an acknowledgement of personal responsibility for sin.

- St. John of Damascus tells us that all the devil can do is suggest; he cannot force us:

    The devils cannot do anything against us without God's permission... All wickedness, all the passions are inspired by them. But listen: God allows them to suggest sin to a person, but they cannot force him to do it. We ourselves are responsible for accepting or rejecting their seductive suggestions.

- Thus, the devil cannot force me to do anything.

- I am responsible.

- *For I know my transgressions and my sin is ever before me.*

- *Against Thee, Thee only have I sinned and done that which is evil in Thy sight.*

- *Wash me and I shall be whiter than snow.*

- *Create in me a clean heart, O God ...*

- *Restore unto me the joy of Thy salvation.*

"HITLER MADE ME DO IT!"

- The Nuremberg trials after World War II served as an example of placing responsibility for actions.

- The trials put an end to passing the buck to Hitler or the government for one's actions.

- They clearly affirmed that wars do not just happen, but are caused by an individual, or group of individuals, making free will decisions for which they must be held responsible.

- No man could say, "Hitler told me to do it."

- The millions who died at Auschwitz were put to death by the Third Reich, yes;

- by the Nazi hierarchy, yes;

- by the orders of Adolph Hitler or of one of his stooges, yes.

- But the man on the scene who pulled the switch or pushed the button or fired the shot—ultimately he must share the blame.

- Who me? Of course not! Hitler made me do it!

- Not any more, said Nuremberg.

- You are responsible. You share the blame.

Why We Do It!

- The Desert Fathers tell a story that helps explain part of what goes on when we deny reality and blame others.

- They describe each person as carrying two bags over his shoulders.

- One bag he carries over his back where he cannot see it.

- That bag contains his own sins.

- The other bag he carries in front of him where he can see it constantly.

- That bag contains the sins of others.

- It is because we very conveniently hide our sins over our backs and can see only the sins of our neighbors that we say, "Who, me?

- I don't need to repent.

- Look at so-and-so's sins.

- If anyone needs to repent, he does!"

- And when we read the newspapers each day and see all the violent things people do, we compare ourselves to those people and, patting ourselves on the back, we say,

- "My, my! I'm certainly not like that!

- I'll have no trouble making it to heaven!"

- In contrast to this, when a person truly knows himself in Christ, he compares himself not to criminals but to Christ, with excuses for his neighbor's faults, but never for his own.

- He keeps praying the prayer of the Publican, "Lord, be merciful to me, the sinner!"

STEALING THE SERMON

- As a lady left church one Sunday, she said to the pastor,

- "My, that was a good sermon. Mrs. So-and-So really needed that.

- Too bad, she wasn't here."

- Later the preacher confided to a friend,

- "I'm afraid that some of the members of my congregation are displeasing the Lord because they're too generous!"

- Seeing the surprised look on the man's face, he continued,

- "This is probably the first time you've ever heard a pastor complain that his parishioners are giving too much.

- But I'm not referring to money;

- I'm speaking of my sermons.

- Some people are giving away too many of my sermons.

- They hear my preaching and say it's very good, but then they conveniently pass it over their shoulders to someone sitting behind them.

- They're blind to their own faults, and they refuse to take God's word personally."

- This is how the devil actually steals God's word from us: when we apply it to others and not to ourselves.

- We need to listen to St. Isaac again, "He who sees his own sins is greater than he who resurrects the dead."

- Who me?

- Of course not! That sermon was meant for so-and-so!

- Was it?

- *For I know my transgressions and my sin (not my neighbor's!) is ever before me.*

"I AM EICHMANN!"

- Evil does not abide in others only; it abides in me.

- Solzhenitsyn once said,

   Evil is real because it is always personal. It does not lie in an impersonal system, nor does it come from impersonal structures. It is found in us, in people who have chosen and continually choose to serve evil.

- Yehiel Dinur -Nazi concentration camp survivor- was a witness during the trial of Adolf Eichmann in Israel.

- Dinur entered the courtroom and stared at the man behind the bulletproof glass—the man who had presided over the slaughter of millions.

- The court was hushed as a victim confronted the butcher of his people.

- Suddenly Dinur began to sob and collapsed to the floor.

- But not out of anger or bitterness.

- As he explained later in an interview, what struck him was a terrifying realization.

- "I was afraid about myself," Dinur said.

- "I saw that *I* am capable to do this....Exactly like him."

- He didn't see before him a monster, a devil with horns and a tail, but another human being like himself.

- In a moment of chilling clarity, Dinur saw the skull beneath the skin.

- "Eichmann," he concluded, "is in all of us."

- Did not Jesus say the same thing:

    All evil things come from within. For out of the heart of man come evil thoughts, fornication, theft, murder, adultery, covetousness, wickedness, deceit, slander, envy, licentiousness, and pride.

- Dostoevsky said once,

- "Remember that you cannot be a judge of anyone.

- For no one can judge a criminal, until he recognizes that he is just such a criminal as the man standing before him,

- and that he perhaps is more than all men to blame for that crime."

- When a person was brought before a judge for sentencing during the Depression because he had stolen a loaf of bread for his starving family,

- Mayor LaGuardia of New York City fined everyone in the courtroom 50 cents for living in a town where one had to steal bread in order to live.

- Evil is always personal.

- It is to be found in each of us.

- *Against Thee, Thee only have I sinned, and done which is evil in Thy sight.*

"I'm Only Human!"

- One night Archie Bunker discovered that in their card games over the years, his wife, Edith, had been letting him win.

- Archie blew his top.

- <u>Archie</u>: That's you all right, Edith the Good.
  You'll stoop to anything to be good.
  You never yell.
  You never swear.
  You never make nobody mad.
  You think it's easy living with a saint?
  Even when you cheat you don't cheat to win.
  You cheat to lose.
  Edith, you ain't human.

- <u>Edith</u>: That's a terrible thing to say, Archie Bunker. I am just as human as you are.

- <u>Archie</u>: Oh yeah...then prove you're just as human as me. Do something rotten.

- How many of us feel, as Archie did, that to be human is to do something rotten?

- Many times we do not seem to be proud of being human.

- We seem to be ashamed of it.

- When we want a way out, we take refuge in our humanity.

- "I'm only human," we say.

- When we want to make excuses for our failures, we usually end up saying that we are only human.

- We do not use our humanity as a challenge to great living.

- Rather we use it as an excuse for whatever weakness we have.

- Every weakness, every mistake, every sin, everything cheap in living, is finally justified on the basis that we are only human.

- But to be truly human is to be like Christ Who was truly God but also truly human, like us in everything except sin.

- So, if we are going to say, "I'm only human,"

- let's say it as we look at the perfect example of what a human can truly be: Jesus Christ!

- Jesus came to show us what it means to be truly human.

- Who me? Of course not!

- I'm only human!

- Was not Jesus human?

- Is not to be truly human to be like Jesus?

I Am Responsible

- To be truly human means that I am responsible!

- The word "responsible" comes from two words: "respond" and "able."

- In other words, I am *able to respond*;

- I am *able to act*.

- I am not a victim of circumstances.

- I am in control.

- I am accountable.

- *Against Thee, Thee only have I sinned and done that which is evil in Thy sight.*

Our Inability To Accept Responsibility

- C.S. Lewis said once,

  Our inability to accept responsibility is the biggest hell that man faces.

- I've seen children playing with one another.

- One would slap the other and say, "I never touched you."

- And the other would say, "You did. I saw you."
- And the reply would be, "It wasn't me. It was my hand."
- The trouble is that we never outgrow this behavior.
- Transactional Analysis came along a few years ago and taught us to say,
- "I didn't do it.
- The parent in me did it.
- The child in me did it."
- As if there is something terribly wrong in saying,
- "I did it.
- I am responsible."
- I like the honesty of Bear Bryant, former Alabama football coach, who said,
- "If anything goes bad, then I did it.
- If anything goes semi-good, then we did it.
- If anything goes real good, then you did it."
- Someone said,
- "Placing the blame is a bad habit, but taking the blame is a sure builder of character."
- *For I know my transgressions and my sin is ever before me.*

WE MAKE CHOICES FOR WHICH WE ARE RESPONSIBLE

- We live in a day when psychology, psychiatry and sociology are constantly trying to reduce our accountability.

- The truth is that we are indeed victims of many forces in life, and no one can tell just how much our own wills are responsible for what we decide to do.

- I don't know just how much we can blame on the anemic genes and chromosomes we inherited,

- or on the fouled up psychic training they foisted on us in our childhood.

- But I am sure of this.

- Somewhere within the personal dynamics of the wrong we do,

- somewhere inside the working of our mind or will,

- we make a choice for which we alone can give an answer.

- We choose, we act, we are accountable, we are responsible.

- Not my father,

- not my mother,

- not my bad childhood.

- not my genes, not my compulsions.

- It's me standing in the need of forgiveness.

- The prodigal son did not blame his father for his condition.

- Instead, he assumed full responsibility for himself when he said, "Father, I have sinned against heaven and before you.

- I am not worthy to be called your son..."

- Because of this confession of personal responsibility, he was gloriously and joyfully forgiven.

- *I recognize my faults,* wrote David.

- *I am always conscious of my sins.*

- *I have sinned against You—only against You.*

- *And done what you consider evil.*

- Who me?

- Yes, Lord, it's me!

- Be merciful to me the sinner!

- *Purge me with hyssop. Wash me, and I shall be whiter than snow.*

MAN: A SELF-EXCUSING ANIMAL

- Man is a self-excusing animal.

- As the only creature capable of doing wrong, man is the

only one capable of telling himself that wrong is right and evil is good.

- Man, the only creature capable of reasoning, is the only creature capable of denying reality, devising all sorts of rationalizations and excuses for what he does.

- Dr. M. Scott Peck, author of the book *The Road Less Traveled*, wrote, "Evil is the persistent refusal of the evil person to face the truth about himself.

- He is constantly scapegoating, laying it on other people, projecting his sins onto others."

- But if man is a self-excusing animal, he is also more than an animal.

- He is created in the image and likeness of God.

- As such he is far more than an animal.

- Animals do not repent, but man can and must repent.

- He can face up to what he is and to what he can become when he receives God's forgiveness.

- For no other creature is destined to be a partaker of God's nature.

- The Apostle John says it clearly,

   "If we say we have no sin, we deceive ourselves and the truth is not in us (I John 1:8)... If we say we have not sinned, we make Him (God) a liar and his word is not in us" (I John 1:10).

- All this passing of the buck - says Apostle John - is nothing but a deceit, a lie, a denial of reality.

- But the Apostle John goes on to say,

- "If we confess our sins, He (God) is faithful and just, and will forgive our sins and cleanse us from all unrighteousness" (I John 1:9).

- Those who deny their sin, their accountability are self-deceived, says the Apostle John. They deny truth

- David was not self-deceived when he said, *Against Thee, Thee only have I sinned and done evil in Thy sight.*

A Statue of Responsibility

- Dr. Viktor Frankl, the famous psychiatrist, said once that there is altogether too much emphasis on liberty and freedom in the United States.

- He suggested that since we have the Statue of Liberty in New York City, we need to erect another statue on the West Coast: a Statue of Responsibility.

- We need to stop talking about "life, liberty and the pursuit of happiness" and start talking about "life, liberty, and the pursuit of responsibility."

- Sin turns us into God-evaders, truth evaders, responsibility evaders.

- When Jesus announced at the Last Supper that one of the disciples would betray Him, they could have said, "Who me?"

- But they didn't.

- Instead they asked,
- "Lord, is it I?"
- Am I what is wrong with the world?
- Am I what is wrong with my home?
- Am I the problem in my fouled-up life and my fouled-up relationships?"
- Don't ask, "How did evil come into this world?" because it comes through you and me.
- *Against Thee, Thee only have I sinned and done evil in Thy sight.*

CHOICES ARE IMPORTANT

- God will not ultimately allow us to evade responsibility.
- St. Paul says in Romans 14:12, "Each of us shall give account of himself to God."
- Our choices are important.
- God does not force us to believe.
- He does not force us to obey.
- But he does hold us responsible for our decisions.
- The existence of heaven and hell is the greatest monument there is to human responsibility.

- It tells us that we must finally be held accountable for our actions, that we are eternally responsible for them.

- Thomas Merton said once,

- "It is only in assuming full responsibility for our world, for our lives, and for ourselves that we can be said to live really for God."

- Accepting personal responsibility is not only God's will for us;

- it is also liberating, empowering, and life-changing.

- Who me?

- Yes, Lord, it's me standing in need of forgiveness.

- *Have mercy on me, O God, according to Thy steadfast love, according to Thy abundant mercy, blot out my transgressions.*

BLAME YOURSELF

- It is only when we accept responsibility for ourselves that we take the first step to betterment.

- You cannot solve a problem unless you take responsibility for it.

- We see it in mental illness.

- A noted psychologist said,

- "My observation is that the patient who condemns himself,

even to the point of thinking he has committed the unpardonable sin, is likely to get well.

- *It is the patient who blames others who does not get well."*

- We see it in the family.

- Nothing heals rifts in family life quicker than for the person who has been selfish or unthoughtful to confess the wrong and apologize.

- As soon as the guilty partner says, "I'm sorry. I was wrong," there is no more misunderstanding.

- It disappears.

- In fact, the wife or husband may even say in return,

- "Oh, no, you're not totally to blame. It was my fault too."

- This is what happens when we accept responsibility for ourselves as mature Christians and seek one another's forgiveness.

- The same thing happens in our relationship to God.

- Refusing to acknowledge our sin, blaming it on others, is one of the greatest barriers that keeps people apart from God and from each other.

- But as soon as we place the blame where it belongs— squarely on our shoulders;

- as soon as we are honest with ourselves, and say "I'm sorry" to the person we have hurt and to our heavenly Father,

- then there is reconciliation;

- then there is forgiveness,

- then there is peace, love, restoration and joy.

- *Fill me with joy and gladness...Restore unto me the joy of Thy salvation.*

THE LIGHTER BURDEN

- One of the Desert Fathers—St. John the Dwarf—warns us:

- "We have put aside the light burden, that is to say, self-accusation, and we have burdened ourselves with a heavy burden, that is to say, self-justification."

- Endless are the ways by which we try to justify ourselves.

- But when the voice of God confronts us with our sin, who can offer God an argument or an excuse?

- Who can justify himself before the Almighty?

- So, what we need to learn is a true, not a morbid, not a co-dependent, but a true self-accusation, like the publican who beat his breast on his knees and prayed, "Lord, be merciful to me the sinner,"

- while the Pharisee kept trying to justify himself before God, "Lord, I fast, I pray, I give to the synagogue. I am not like other people."

- It was the publican, who accused himself, who was justified in God's eyes, not the Pharisee who was blaming others and trying to justify himself.

- Indeed, the lighter burden is self-accusation: to accuse oneself before God. The heavy burden is trying to justify oneself before God and the world.

- Jesus came to set us free from the heavy burden of trying to justify ourselves.

- "A man who sins and repents is preferred by God than one who does not sin and does not repent," wrote St. Theophan the Recluse.

- Who me?

- Yes, Lord, it's me, standing in the need of forgiveness.

- *Have mercy on me, O God, according to Thy steadfast love; according to Thy abundant mercy, blot out my transgressions.*

PRIDE EDITS TRUTH

- Friedrich Nietzsche, the German philosopher, explained what goes on when we try to justify ourselves. He wrote,

- "Pride and memory had an argument.

- Memory said, 'It happened thus and so!'

- Pride replied, 'Oh, but it couldn't have been like that!'

- and memory gave in to pride."

- So it is with us.

- Memory gives in to pride again and again.

- Most of the pictures we recall from the past have been retouched.

- Most of the scripts we can quote from old conversations have been edited by pride.

- Memory remembers reality but pride steps in to edit and distort the truth even to the point of trying to justify ourselves before God.

- Someone said, "Maturity consists in no longer being taken in by yourself."

WHEN TWO PEOPLE HAVE A QUARREL

- Here is an example.

- If two people have a quarrel, and come separately to tell you about it, you will often notice that their respective accounts of what happened differ, sometimes to a surprising extent.

- This is not necessarily because one of them is telling lies, or both of them,

- but because pride steps in through repression and they fail to remember the weak points in their case; each remembers only the strong points.

- Thus pride steps in to distort memory.

- This is how the devil works to keep us from accusing ourselves honestly in order to receive God's forgiveness.

- This is the lighter burden.

- Satan keeps trying to place on us constantly the unbearable burden of trying to justify ourselves.

- It is only when we face the facts about ourselves honestly that there can be healing and new life.

- When we see ourselves for what we really are; when we are ashamed of ourselves and have difficulty accepting ourselves,

- then we can be sure of one thing:

- *God will accept us. God will forgive us.* About nothing is Jesus more emphatic.

- "Him who comes to me, I will in no way cast out," He said.

- "One truly repentant sinner is greater than 10,000 righteous men," said St. Isaac the Syrian.

- Why? St. Isaac answers,

- "Because such a sinner is reborn and transfigured; Christ's resurrection is alive and active in him."

"FATHER, I HAVE SINNED."

- Jesus once told a story about a boy who ran away from responsibility.

- But, "When he came to himself," he went home to his father and said, "Father, I have sinned..."

- He didn't say, "Father, you're to blame."

- He didn't say, "Father, my friends led me astray."

- He didn't say, "Father, my older brother always picked on me."

- No, he said, "Father, I have sinned. I am responsible,"

- and his father threw his arms around him and said,

- "My son was dead, and is alive again; he was lost and is found" (Luke 15:24).

- A new chapter of his life began the very moment he accepted responsibility for himself and said, "*I* have sinned."

- A new chapter can begin for you, too, if, bidding good-bye to self-excuse, self-pity, denial, pride, scapegoating, self-defense, passing the buck, you will face the facts about yourself, get right down to them instead of running away from them;

- and say to yourself,

- "Yes, that is the kind of person I am, that is the sort of thing I am capable of doing and have done, but, by the grace of God, I can be different, and I will be."

- Someone once said,

- "The person who blames others for his problems hasn't begun his education.

- The person who blames himself has begun his education.

- And the person who blames no one but himself has finished his education."

- An old Hasidic story says that God never told us how life began, but He does tell us how life can begin again, here and now, i.e., through honest repentance and confession:

- *Against Thee, Thee only have I sinned...*

- *Close your eyes to my sins and wipe away all my evil...*

- *Create a pure heart in me, O God, and put a new and loyal spirit in me.*

- This is how new life begins!

DAVID'S GREATNESS: HIS CONFESSION

- David was Israel's greatest king, *a man after God's own heart,* prototype of the Messiah.

- He was a giant killer, a bold warrior, a masterful general and strategist.

- He was also the one who united Israel's twelve tribes and ushered in Israel's golden age.

- But his greatness was not in his military prowess nor in his statesmanship.

- For, you see, David was also a great sinner.

- He enticed Bathseba, committed adultery with her, then tried to conceal his sin by having her husband murdered.

- But when confronted by God's prophet—Nathan—David openly acknowledged and confessed his sin.

- To express his repentance, he wrote Psalm 51 which is read in almost all Orthodox worship services because it is one of the greatest expressions of repentance and confession ever written.

- Therein lay David's greatness.

- Not that he sinned, but that he did not hide it.

- He did not let pride edit memory and distort reality.

- He did not say, "Who me?"

- He acknowledged his sin.

- He confessed it and begged God's mercy.

- I *have sinned against You, only against You, and done what You consider evil.*

- This was his true greatness.

- It can be ours, too!

- For the blood of Jesus cleanses only sins—not excuses.

WHERE DOES THE BUCK STOP ULTIMATELY?

- President Truman had a sign on his desk that said, "The buck stops here."

- But is that where the buck ultimately stops?

- On your desk or mine?

- No! The buck really stops at the cross of our Lord Jesus!

- He accepted "the buck" for all of us.

- "God made Him who knew no sin at all to be sin for us, that we might be made the righteousness of God in Him" (2 Cor.5:21).

- He paid the penalty for sin so that we might be forgiven and have newness of life, and go on to become "partakers of divine nature",

- but first we must come to him in repentance.

- It all begins with acknowledging our sinfulness as did David and the publican:

- *Lord, be merciful to me, the sinner.*

- At Phoenix House, the highly regarded drug-rehabilitation center in New York,

- a typical therapy group will start out by listening quietly to all the "victim" chatter of a recently arrived addict.

- Then someone will say something like this:

- "It wasn't your mother or society or even the pushers who put the needle in your arm. You did."

- And therapy starts from there.

Admit It!

- The first step in solving a problem is to admit you have a problem.

- Then call it by its proper name. It means saying,

- "I have sinned.

- I didn't tell the truth.

- I cheated.

- I can't get along with that person."

- That is what David—a man after God's own heart—did.

- He told the Lord,

- *I finally admitted all my sins to you and stopped trying to hide them... And you forgave me* (Psalm 32:5).

- *A sacrifice acceptable to God is a broken spirit, a broken and contrite heart, O God, you will not despise.*

- My biggest problem isn't somebody else.

- It's me.

- Your biggest problem isn't somebody else.

- It's you.

- We're not just victims; we're sinners.

- God's law shows you and me our sin, writes Paul in Romans, "so that every mouth may be silenced and the whole world held accountable to God" (3:19).

- God crashes the pity party and interrupts the blame game to tell us,

- "You are to blame.

- Admit it.

- Accept responsibility for yourself.

- Repent! For the kingdom of God is at hand."

COMING FACE-TO-FACE WITH GOD

- When we come face to face with God, we stop trying to excuse ourselves by blaming others.

- Instead we confess our wrongdoing openly.

- Like Isaiah when he had a vision of standing before God's throne, we say,

- *Woe is me! I am ruined. For I am a man of unclean lips, and I live among people of unclean lips, and my eyes have seen the King, the Lord Almighty* (Isaiah 6:5).

FROM THE CANON OF ST. ANDREW OF CRETE

- The Canon of St. Andrew of Crete that is used during Lent is filled with open confessions of guilt—no excuses, no rationalizations, no justifications, no scapegoating, no passing the buck.

- Here are some of the prayers:

   More than all men have I sinned; I alone have sinned against Thee. But as God take pity on Thy creation, O Savior.

   I have adorned the idol of my flesh with a many-colored coat of shameful thoughts, and I am condemned.

   Adam was justly banished from Eden because he disobeyed one commandment of thine, O my Savior. What then shall I suffer, for disobeying many, for I am always rejecting the words of Life?...I have rivaled in transgression Adam, the first born man, and I have found myself stripped naked of God, of the eternal Kingdom and its joy, because of my sins.

   ...Like the harlot I cry to Thee: I have sinned, I alone have sinned against Thee. Accept my tears also as a sweet ointment, O Savior.

   Like the Publican I cry to Thee: Be merciful, O Savior, be merciful to me. For no child of Adam has ever sinned against Thee as I have sinned.

HE STOLE HEAVEN

- The thief on the cross next to Jesus acknowledged his sin and heard Jesus say to him, "Truly I say to you, today you will be with me in paradise."

- With this statement of confession, John Chrysostom wrote, "the thief sprang off the cross right into paradise."

- He ended up a real thief by stealing heaven itself!

- A beautiful prayer of accepting blame for our sins is one we pray at every Presanctified Liturgy:

  O Lord and Master of my life, take from me the spirit of sloth, faintheartedness, lust for power and idle talk. But give Thy servant the spirit of chastity, humility, patience and love. Yea, O Lord and King, grant me to see my own errors and not judge my brother, for Thou art blessed unto ages of ages. Amen.

  -St. Ephrem the Syrian

- *Yea, Lord, grant me to see my own sins, and not to judge my brother.*

- These words are a call to repentance.

- May our response be like that of David when he said at a crucial moment in his life:

- *I recognize my faults,*

- *I am always conscious of my sins.*

- *I have sinned against you, God, and done what You consider evil...*

- *Remove my sin, and I will be clean;*

- *wash me and I will be whiter than snow...*

- *Create a pure heart in me, O God, and put a new and loyal spirit in me.*

- *Give me again the joy that comes from Your salvation, and make me willing to obey You.*

When Is Man A Failure?

- Man is never a failure until he blames someone else.

- When a person plays the Blame Game, it's a sure sign it's time for him to play the Confession Game, come clean with God—and be honest with himself.

- If you have not come to an awareness of your sinfulness, Jesus cannot come to you, because He came to save not the righteous, but sinners (Mt. 9:13).

- A Church father says,

- "How does a person who is unrepentant and always blaming others differ from a demon?"

- The answer is he doesn't!

- We need to take a good look at ourselves by looking into the mirror of God's word, to see what is reflected back to us,

- to cease trying to justify ourselves,

- to admit our sinfulness and let God justify us.

- *I have sinned against You, and done what is evil in your sight.*

- Let us now pray together David's prayer of confession in Psalm 51 where, instead of blaming others, he accepts full responsibility for his sins and pleads God's forgiveness.

- Let us make it our personal confession:

    *Be merciful to me, O God, because of your constant love.
    Because of your great mercy wipe away my sin!
    Wash away all my evil and make me clean from my sin!
    I recognize my faults;
    I am always conscious of my sins.*

    I have sinned against you—only against you—and done what you consider evil.

    *So you are right in judging me; you are justified in condemning me.
    I have been evil from the time I was born;
    from the day of my birth I have been sinful...*

    *Remove my sin, and I will be clean;
    wash me, and I will be whiter than snow.
    Let me hear the sounds of joy and gladness;
    and though you have crushed me and broken me,
    I will be happy once again.
    Close your eyes to my sins and wipe out all my evil.*

    *Create a pure heart in me, O God,
    and put a new and loyal spirit in me.*

Do not banish me from your presence;
do not take your holy spirit away from me.
Give me again the joy that comes from your
salvation, and make me willing to obey you...

You do not want sacrifices, or I would offer them;
you are not pleased with burnt offerings.
My sacrifice is a humble spirit, O God;
you will not reject a humble and repentant heart.

Prayer

I look to You, O Lord and I say, "Who me, Lord?"
and You say, "Yes, you, my son, my daughter.
You are the one who has left home and traveled away
into the far country of sin.
You are the one I am waiting for
with arms nailed to the cross.
You are the one I am seeking.
You are the one upon whom I can hardly
wait to bestow my grace and forgiveness.
But first you must stop making excuses
and passing the buck.
You must say like the prodigal,
"I have sinned." Then when you ask,
"Who, me, Lord?" I will say to you,
"Yes, my son, my daughter, Yes! You!
Come inherit the kingdom prepared for you
from the foundation of the world."
Amen.

This is one of the many books published by:

LIGHT & LIFE PUBLISHING COMPANY

P.O. Box 26421

Minneapolis, MN 55426-00421

Telephone: 612-925-3888

E-Mail: info@light-n-life.com

Toll-Free Fax (U.S. and Canada Only): 1-888-925-3918

International Fax: 1-612-925-3918

YES! Please send me a free catalog listing your complete selection of Orthodox Christian books.

Name: _____

Street Address: _____

City, State, Zip: _____

Telephone: (___) _____

LIGHT & LIFE PUBLISHING COMPANY
P.O. Box 26421
Minneapolis, MN 55426-0421

Visit our web site: http://www.light-n-life.com